SUPERMAN: A NEW DAWM MOVIE REVIEW

James Gunn's Vision for the Iconic Hero Reaches New Heights in the 2025 Reboot

Sara J. Jones

Copyright © 2024 by [*Sara J. Jones*]

First Edition: 2024

All rights reserved. No part of this book may be reproduced or transmitted in any form or by any means, electronic or mechanical, including photocopying, recording, or by an information storage and retrieval system, without the permission in writing form from the publisher.

PUBLISHED BY:

Sara J. Jones

Table of Content

Introduction 6

Overview of the Movie 6

Chapter 1 11

Director and Vision 11

    James Gunn's Direction 11

    Approach to the Superman Mythos 13

Chapter 2 19

Cast and Performances: A Deep Dive into the Superman Legacy 19

    David Corenswet as Clark Kent/Superman 19

    Rachel Brosnahan as Lois Lane 21

    Nicholas Hoult as Lex Luthor 23

    The Interplay Between the Trio 25

Chapter 3 27

Plot and Themes 27

    Balancing Kryptonian Heritage and Human Upbringing 28

    The Weight of Legacy 29

    Emotional and Vulnerable Superman 30

    Love and Connection 31

    Struggles with Self-Doubt 32

    Resilience and Hope 32

Chapter 4 35

Visuals and Effects: A Deep Dive into "Superman (2025)"

.... 35

    Special Effects Focus 36

    IMAX Experience 38

    Bridging Spectacle and Emotion 41

Chapter 5 44

Role in the DC Universe: Chapter One: Gods and Monsters

.... 44

    Chapter One: Gods and Monsters 45

    Rebooting the Franchise 46

    Integration with Other DC Properties 48

    Challenges and Opportunities 49

    Establishing a Legacy 50

Chapter 6 52

Anticipation and First Impressions 52

    Teaser Trailer Breakdown 52

    Audience Expectations 55

conclusion 60

    Summary of Excitement for the Film 60

    Predictions for Impact on the Superman Legacy 63

Introduction
Overview of the Movie

Superman has long been a symbol of hope, courage, and resilience, and the upcoming movie slated for release on July 11, 2025, seeks to reignite this iconic legacy. Directed by James Gunn, this film marks the beginning of a new chapter in the DC Universe's evolving cinematic saga. Known for his deft storytelling and ability to balance humor, heart, and high-stakes action, Gunn's vision for Superman promises to delve deeper into the dual identity of Clark Kent. With a fresh approach, the film explores the struggles of a man torn between two worlds: his Kryptonian heritage and his human upbringing.

The narrative will focus on Superman's quest to reconcile his extraordinary abilities with the simple, profound lessons he learned growing up in Smallville, Kansas. This duality is at the core of the character's appeal, offering audiences a chance to connect with a hero who embodies both immense power and relatable vulnerability. As the inaugural installment of DC Studios' "Chapter One: Gods and Monsters," this movie not only aims to reset the Superman franchise but also serves as a foundational piece for the broader cinematic universe that is being meticulously crafted.

Adding to the anticipation is the promise of a grounded, emotional story that maintains the grandeur associated with the Man of Steel. By placing an emphasis on his humanity, the film seeks to bring a fresh perspective to a character that has graced comic books, television screens, and theaters for over eight decades. In this iteration, Superman's struggles with identity, morality, and belonging will be brought to life through an intimate yet epic storytelling lens, making it one of the most anticipated superhero films in years.

Release Details

Superman's return to the big screen is scheduled for a global release on July 11, 2025. The film will premiere in theaters worldwide, including special IMAX screenings that promise a visually stunning experience. Fans are already abuzz with excitement following the release of the teaser trailer, which dropped in December 2024, offering a glimpse into the emotional depth and visual spectacle that awaits.

The production team has placed significant emphasis on ensuring top-tier visual effects, dedicating an entire year to perfecting them. This meticulous approach underscores the film's ambition to deliver a Superman story that is both visually and narratively unparalleled. The use of cutting-edge technology aims to enhance the cinematic experience, immersing audiences in Superman's world like never before.

David Corenswet, who steps into the iconic role of Clark Kent/Superman, has already garnered attention for his striking resemblance to previous portrayals and his earnest dedication to the character. He is joined by Rachel Brosnahan as Lois Lane, whose sharp wit and dynamic presence promise to bring new energy to Superman's longtime partner and love interest. Nicholas Hoult, as the enigmatic Lex Luthor, adds another layer of intrigue to the cast, setting the stage for an engaging conflict between hero and villain.

This movie is not just another addition to the DC cinematic lineup; it's a significant cultural moment. Positioned as the cornerstone of a revamped DC Universe, the film represents a bold attempt to reimagine Superman for a new generation. By balancing the character's traditional values with modern sensibilities, it aims to resonate with longtime fans while captivating a fresh audience.

As the release date approaches, the buzz surrounding the movie continues to grow, fueled by high expectations and the passionate support of Superman enthusiasts around the globe. Whether it's through its heartfelt story, its stellar cast, or its groundbreaking visuals, this Superman film promises to be a defining entry in the superhero genre. With its release, audiences will once again be reminded why the Man of Steel remains one of the most beloved and enduring characters in the history of popular culture.

Chapter 1
Director and Vision

James Gunn's Direction

When it was announced that James Gunn would helm the new Superman film slated for release on July 11, 2025, excitement and speculation ran high. Gunn, known for his ability to blend heartfelt storytelling with humor and action, brings a fresh perspective to the Man of Steel. Gunn's previous successes with the Guardians of the Galaxy series and The Suicide Squad showcased his ability to balance character-driven narratives with visually striking, high-octane sequences. For Superman, Gunn has promised a return to the core essence of the character while reimagining him for a new generation.

Gunn's direction emphasizes depth and relatability, qualities often overlooked in larger-than-life superhero films. By focusing on Superman's emotional and psychological journey, Gunn seeks to explore not just the hero's powers but his humanity. In a recent interview, Gunn highlighted his desire to portray Superman as a "beacon of hope," but one who is not immune to doubts and struggles. This nuanced approach aims to connect audiences with Superman's internal conflicts and moral dilemmas, making the character more approachable without diminishing his iconic status.

Another hallmark of Gunn's direction is his attention to detail and collaborative spirit. He has a proven track record of crafting ensemble casts, creating fully realized characters whose arcs resonate within the larger narrative. While Superman is undoubtedly the focus, Gunn's touch ensures that supporting characters like Lois Lane, Lex Luthor, and others will be given their own time to shine, contributing to a richer cinematic experience. The interplay between these characters is poised to reflect Gunn's knack for delivering dynamic relationships that serve as the emotional backbone of his stories.

Gunn also excels in creating visually unique worlds that complement his storytelling. For Superman, he has emphasized the importance of visual effects and cinematography in enhancing the narrative. With a production schedule allowing for a year-long refinement of visual effects, Gunn is aiming for a film that is as visually spectacular as it is emotionally impactful. The choice to release the movie in IMAX underscores the ambition to provide a grand, immersive experience worthy of Superman's legendary stature.

Approach to the Superman Mythos

Superman has been a cultural icon for over 85 years, and each iteration of the character has reflected the era in which it was created. Gunn's Superman seeks to honor this legacy while charting new territory. Central to his approach is the exploration of Clark Kent's dual heritage—his Kryptonian lineage and his upbringing in Smallville, Kansas. This dichotomy forms the heart of the character and serves as the lens through which Gunn will examine Superman's identity.

In this version, Superman is portrayed as a figure caught between two worlds, grappling with his responsibilities as Earth's protector and his desire to lead a normal life. Gunn's emphasis on Clark's human upbringing promises to highlight themes of compassion, humility, and resilience. By rooting the character in his small-town values, Gunn underscores the importance of Superman's humanity as the source of his strength. This human element, often overshadowed by his superhuman abilities, will take center stage in Gunn's narrative.

At the same time, Gunn is keenly aware of Superman's Kryptonian heritage and the weight it carries. By delving into the legacy of Krypton, the film promises to offer a richer understanding of Clark's origins and the challenges of living up to the ideals of a lost civilization. This exploration of Krypton's culture, science, and moral philosophy will provide a nuanced backdrop to Superman's journey, framing his struggle to reconcile the values of two vastly different worlds.

Gunn's approach also seeks to address the timeless debate about Superman's place in a world increasingly cynical about heroes. In a landscape where antiheroes often dominate, Gunn aims to reestablish Superman as an unambiguous force for good. However, this idealism will not come without challenges. The film is expected to portray a Superman who is acutely aware of the complexities and imperfections of humanity. This awareness, rather than diminishing his optimism, strengthens his resolve to inspire others to be better. Gunn's Superman is not naïve but steadfast, a hero who embodies hope precisely because he understands the cost of maintaining it.

One of the most anticipated aspects of Gunn's take on the mythos is his treatment of the supporting cast. Lois Lane, portrayed by Rachel Brosnahan, is set to be a formidable counterpart to Superman, bringing intelligence, wit, and emotional depth to the story. As a renowned journalist, Lois represents truth and justice in her own right, complementing Superman's ideals while challenging him to stay grounded. Similarly, Nicholas Hoult's Lex Luthor is expected to offer a more layered depiction of the classic villain. Gunn has hinted at exploring Lex's motivations and moral ambiguity, providing a foil that challenges Superman on intellectual and ideological levels.

Gunn's ability to weave humor and heart into his narratives is another element that will shape his approach to the Superman mythos. While the character has traditionally been associated with earnestness, Gunn's knack for balancing levity with gravitas could bring a fresh dynamic to the story. This balance is particularly important in making Superman's struggles relatable without undermining his role as a larger-than-life hero.

Furthermore, Gunn's decision to situate this film within the broader context of the new DC Universe adds an additional layer of intrigue. As the inaugural chapter of Gods and Monsters, this film will set the tone for the franchise's direction. Gunn's vision for Superman as a cornerstone of this universe signals a return to cohesive world-building, with the character's ideals serving as a foundation for the stories to come. The title of the chapter itself hints at the exploration of divine and monstrous elements within the DC Universe, positioning Superman as a bridge between these extremes.

Finally, Gunn's approach to the Superman mythos emphasizes the universal appeal of the character. By focusing on themes of identity, belonging, and hope, the film seeks to resonate with audiences across cultures and generations. Superman's story is, at its core, a tale of finding one's place in the world and choosing to make it better. Gunn's direction ensures that this timeless message will remain at the heart of the narrative, even as it is reimagined for contemporary audiences.

James Gunn's direction and approach to the Superman mythos promise a fresh yet faithful reimagining of the iconic hero. By blending emotional depth, character-driven storytelling, and stunning visuals, Gunn aims to create a film that honors Superman's legacy while making him relevant for a new era. With a focus on Clark Kent's dual heritage, the complexities of his humanity, and his unwavering optimism, Gunn's Superman is poised to inspire audiences and reaffirm the character's status as a symbol of hope and justice. As the cornerstone of the new DC Universe, this film has the potential to redefine Superman's place in pop culture and set a new standard for superhero storytelling.

Chapter 2
Cast and Performances: A Deep Dive into the Superman Legacy

The cast of the upcoming Superman film, set to release on July 11, 2025, is one of its most anticipated elements, promising a refreshing take on the iconic characters that have shaped pop culture for decades. This section delves into the casting choices of David Corenswet as Clark Kent/Superman, Rachel Brosnahan as Lois Lane, and Nicholas Hoult as Lex Luthor, analyzing their potential to redefine these legendary roles while maintaining the essence of what makes them timeless.

David Corenswet as Clark Kent/Superman

David Corenswet's casting as Clark Kent/Superman has been a focal point of discussion among fans and critics alike. Known for his charming yet grounded performances in projects like The Politician and Hollywood, Corenswet brings a fresh yet familiar aura to the Man of Steel. One of the key aspects of Superman is his dual identity—a humble, earnest farm boy from Smallville and an all-powerful alien beacon of hope. Corenswet's ability to embody vulnerability while exuding confidence makes him an intriguing choice for the role.

Superman's characterization hinges on his relatability despite his godlike abilities. Corenswet's previous roles demonstrate his skill at portraying emotionally nuanced characters. His warm smile and sincere demeanor echo the legacy of Christopher Reeve's Superman, which many consider the gold standard. At the same time, Corenswet's youthful energy could infuse the character with a modern edge, making him relatable to contemporary audiences.

Moreover, this iteration of Superman will reportedly focus on his struggles to reconcile his Kryptonian heritage with his human upbringing. This narrative arc requires an actor capable of navigating complex emotions, and Corenswet's history of tackling layered characters suggests he's up to the task. His physical transformation for the role also underscores his commitment; early glimpses reveal a physique befitting the world's strongest superhero, ensuring he embodies the role both emotionally and physically.

Rachel Brosnahan as Lois Lane

Rachel Brosnahan's selection as Lois Lane has been met with widespread excitement, largely due to her critically acclaimed portrayal of Midge Maisel in The Marvelous Mrs. Maisel. Lois Lane, the intrepid journalist of the Daily Planet, is much more than Superman's love interest. She's a fearless, sharp-witted reporter who often serves as the moral compass and heart of the story. Brosnahan's knack for portraying independent, strong-willed characters makes her a natural fit for the role.

Lois Lane's character has evolved significantly over the decades, moving from a damsel in distress to a formidable force in her own right. Brosnahan's past performances indicate that she can bring a layered portrayal of Lois—balancing vulnerability with unshakable determination. Her quick wit and comedic timing, as showcased in The Marvelous Mrs. Maisel, align perfectly with the sharp, sometimes sarcastic banter that has historically defined Lois's interactions with Clark Kent.

What sets this casting apart is Brosnahan's ability to convey both professional ambition and emotional depth. Lois Lane often serves as a lens through which audiences understand Superman's humanity, and Brosnahan's emotional range ensures she can hold her own in scenes alongside Corenswet. Early reports suggest that this film will explore the dynamic between Lois and Clark as more than a love story, delving into their partnership as equals in their fight for justice. Brosnahan's portrayal is likely to redefine the character for a new generation, emphasizing her role as a journalist who risks everything to uncover the truth.

Nicholas Hoult as Lex Luthor

Nicholas Hoult's casting as Lex Luthor is arguably the boldest choice among the trio. Known for his versatility in roles ranging from Warm Bodies to The Great, Hoult's acting prowess and ability to transform himself make him an inspired pick for Superman's archenemy. Lex Luthor is a character of immense complexity—a genius billionaire whose intellect and charisma are matched only by his deep-seated insecurities and obsession with Superman.

Hoult's performance as Peter III in The Great showcases his ability to bring depth to morally ambiguous characters. While often depicted as comically inept, Hoult's Peter reveals flashes of cunning and ruthlessness beneath his veneer of charm—qualities that are essential for portraying a compelling Lex Luthor. This duality could make Hoult's Lex one of the most fascinating interpretations yet, capturing both the character's public persona as a philanthropist and his private vendetta against Superman.

Lex Luthor's animosity toward Superman is often rooted in his belief that the hero represents an existential threat to humanity's autonomy. This film's emphasis on Superman's struggle to balance his alien heritage with his human upbringing sets the stage for a Lex Luthor who views himself as humanity's last line of defense. Hoult's ability to convey intellectual arrogance and emotional vulnerability ensures he can navigate these themes with nuance.

Additionally, Hoult's physical transformation for the role—potentially shedding his typically boyish charm for a more menacing and imposing demeanor—will further solidify his presence as a formidable antagonist. Early hints suggest this version of Lex Luthor will be more grounded and emotionally complex than previous cinematic iterations, allowing Hoult to bring his signature depth to the role.

The Interplay Between the Trio

While each actor's individual performance will undoubtedly shine, the success of the film hinges on the chemistry between Clark Kent, Lois Lane, and Lex Luthor. Superman's relationship with Lois serves as the emotional core of the story, while his rivalry with Lex provides its dramatic tension. Corenswet and Brosnahan's ability to create a believable and compelling partnership is crucial for grounding the film's more fantastical elements. Their shared scenes need to reflect mutual respect and admiration, offering a modern take on the classic dynamic.

Similarly, the interactions between Corenswet's Superman and Hoult's Lex Luthor must capture the philosophical and emotional clash at the heart of their rivalry. If Hoult's Lex is portrayed as a mirror to Superman—a man who, despite his brilliance, succumbs to fear and jealousy—it could elevate the narrative beyond a simple good-versus-evil conflict. The tension between them should reflect broader themes of power, morality, and humanity's capacity for both greatness and self-destruction.

The casting choices of David Corenswet, Rachel Brosnahan, and Nicholas Hoult promise a revitalized take on Superman's iconic characters. Each actor brings unique strengths that align with their respective roles, offering the potential to balance the grandeur of superhero storytelling with grounded, emotionally resonant performances. As the cornerstone of DC's cinematic reboot, their portrayals will not only redefine these beloved characters but also set the tone for the franchise's future. With a talented cast ready to breathe new life into these roles, the upcoming Superman film is poised to become a defining moment in superhero cinema.

Chapter 3
Plot and Themes

The upcoming Superman film, slated for release on July 11, 2025, presents an opportunity to delve deeper into the nuanced character of Clark Kent/Kal-El. While Superman is often seen as a near-invincible force of hope, the film's focus on balancing his Kryptonian heritage with his human upbringing introduces a profoundly personal and relatable dimension to the Man of Steel. Furthermore, the exploration of his emotional vulnerability adds depth to the character, showcasing a side of Superman that has often been overshadowed by his godlike abilities. This thematic interplay promises a fresh perspective, marking a significant evolution in how Superman is portrayed on screen.

Balancing Kryptonian Heritage and Human Upbringing

Superman's dual identity as Kal-El of Krypton and Clark Kent of Earth has always been central to his story. This dichotomy forms the crux of his character, symbolizing the struggle to reconcile two vastly different worlds. Raised by Jonathan and Martha Kent in the idyllic small town of Smallville, Clark grows up surrounded by love, moral guidance, and the values of humility and kindness. His human upbringing instills in him a sense of responsibility and compassion, which serves as the foundation of his heroic persona.

However, the knowledge of his alien origins often weighs heavily on Clark. The discovery of his Kryptonian heritage—a technologically advanced but ultimately doomed civilization—adds layers of complexity to his identity. The upcoming film appears poised to examine this internal conflict more deeply. Rather than presenting his Kryptonian side as a source of superiority or detachment, it is likely to be framed as a part of his heritage that he must embrace and integrate into his life on Earth. This balancing act is not merely about reconciling two cultures but also about accepting himself fully.

The tension between his two identities also mirrors the broader immigrant experience. Superman's story has often been interpreted as an allegory for the challenges faced by those who navigate multiple cultural identities. In this sense, the film has the potential to resonate with audiences on a deeply personal level, exploring themes of belonging, identity, and the universal desire to find one's place in the world.

The Weight of Legacy
Another compelling aspect of Superman's dual heritage is the legacy of Krypton. The advanced but flawed society of Krypton serves as a cautionary tale, a reminder of the consequences of hubris and environmental neglect. Kal-El's survival is not just a twist of fate but also a charge to ensure

that the mistakes of Krypton are not repeated on Earth. This responsibility often conflicts with the simpler, more grounded life Clark longs for as a human. The film's exploration of this theme is expected to highlight the emotional toll of carrying such a burden, adding a layer of gravitas to the character's journey.

Emotional and Vulnerable Superman

One of the most exciting aspects of the upcoming film is its emphasis on Superman's emotional vulnerability. While his physical invincibility often dominates his portrayal, his internal struggles and emotional depth are what make him truly relatable. By focusing on these aspects, the film aims to present a Superman who is not only heroic but also profoundly human.

Superman's emotional vulnerability often stems from his relationships and his moral dilemmas. His bond with his adoptive parents, Jonathan and Martha Kent, is a cornerstone of his emotional world. Their teachings and sacrifices shape his moral compass, and their loss—a recurring element in Superman lore—often serves as a poignant reminder of his human fragility. The film is likely to explore how these relationships continue to influence him, even as he grapples with the loneliness of being the last son of Krypton.

Love and Connection

Lois Lane, the intrepid journalist and Clark's love interest, is another pivotal figure in his life. Their relationship has always been a blend of admiration, respect, and deep emotional connection. In the context of a more vulnerable Superman, Lois is expected to play a significant role as a source of strength and grounding. Her ability to see and love Clark for who he truly is—beyond his powers—offers a counterbalance to the isolation he often feels.

The film's portrayal of these relationships is critical to its exploration of Superman's emotional landscape. They provide the audience with a window into his humanity, reminding us that even the most powerful beings are shaped by their connections to others.

Struggles with Self-Doubt

Superman's emotional vulnerability also manifests in his struggles with self-doubt. Despite his incredible abilities, he often questions whether he is doing enough or if he is worthy of the trust and admiration bestowed upon him. This internal conflict is particularly resonant in a world where the lines between right and wrong are increasingly blurred. By showcasing these moments of doubt, the film has the opportunity to present a Superman who is not just an ideal to aspire to but also a reflection of our own insecurities and fears.

Resilience and Hope

At its core, Superman's story is one of resilience and hope. His ability to rise above his struggles and inspire others is what makes him a true hero. The film's focus on his emotional journey is not just about highlighting his vulnerabilities but also about showcasing his strength in overcoming them. This balance between vulnerability and resilience is what makes Superman a timeless character.

In portraying a more emotionally nuanced Superman, the film also aligns with contemporary storytelling trends that prioritize character depth and authenticity. By allowing Superman to be vulnerable, the filmmakers are acknowledging that even the most iconic heroes are not immune to the complexities of the human experience. This approach not only enhances the character's relatability but also reinforces the idea that strength and vulnerability are not mutually exclusive.

The upcoming Superman film's exploration of his Kryptonian heritage and human upbringing, along with his emotional vulnerability, promises to offer a fresh and deeply engaging take on the character. By delving into these themes, the film has the potential to redefine Superman for a new generation, emphasizing his humanity as much as his heroism. This nuanced portrayal not only enriches the character but also reaffirms the enduring appeal of

Superman as a symbol of hope, resilience, and the enduring quest for identity and belonging.

Chapter 4
Visuals and Effects: A Deep Dive into "Superman (2025)"

The world of cinema has always relied on visual storytelling to captivate audiences, and superhero movies, in particular, demand an unparalleled level of excellence in their special effects. James Gunn's Superman (2025) is no exception. Positioned as a flagship title in the revamped DC Universe, the film has promised to deliver a visual spectacle that not only showcases Superman's extraordinary abilities but also immerses the audience in a world where the balance between Kryptonian grandeur and human vulnerability is rendered with stunning precision. This essay delves into the two critical aspects of the film's visual and special effects: the focus on groundbreaking technology and artistry in special effects and the immersive experience brought to life by IMAX screenings.

Special Effects Focus

The special effects in superhero films often serve as the backbone of their storytelling, creating believable depictions of the impossible. For Superman (2025), the production team has committed an entire year to perfecting its visual effects—a testament to their dedication to achieving excellence. The focus is not merely on creating visually stunning sequences but on crafting effects that resonate with the emotional and narrative core of the film.

Superman's iconic powers, such as flight, super strength, and heat vision, demand a delicate balance between realism and grandeur. The challenge lies in presenting these abilities in a way that feels organic to the character while still pushing the boundaries of cinematic spectacle. Early glimpses from behind-the-scenes footage suggest a meticulous approach to motion capture and CGI integration. For instance, Superman's flight sequences have reportedly been enhanced using advanced simulation techniques that capture the nuances of movement, wind resistance, and light interaction, ensuring that the audience perceives them as both awe-inspiring and physically plausible.

Another area of focus has been the depiction of Krypton and its technology. The film's design team has drawn inspiration from both classic Superman lore and modern scientific concepts to create a vision of Kryptonian technology that feels futuristic yet grounded. This includes intricate holographic displays, adaptive architecture, and materials that mimic the properties of advanced alloys—all rendered with painstaking attention to detail. These elements are not just visual flourishes but integral to the storytelling, providing insight into Superman's heritage and the legacy of his home planet.

The adversaries in the film, particularly Lex Luthor and potential Kryptonian threats, are also expected to benefit from groundbreaking effects. Whether it's the menacing aura of Lex's advanced weaponry or the raw power of a Kryptonian duel, the visual effects team has emphasized the importance of weight and impact. The use of practical effects, combined with CGI, aims to create a visceral experience where every punch, blast, and collision feels consequential. This approach aligns with James Gunn's commitment to blending spectacle with substance, ensuring that the action sequences are not merely flashy but emotionally charged.

IMAX Experience

The decision to release Superman (2025) in IMAX underscores the film's ambition to offer an unparalleled cinematic experience. IMAX technology has long been celebrated for its ability to immerse audiences in the narrative by enhancing visual clarity, depth, and scale. For a film like Superman (2025), which hinges on the grandeur of its visuals and the emotional resonance of its story, IMAX provides the perfect platform to elevate these elements.

One of the most significant advantages of IMAX is its expanded aspect ratio, which allows filmmakers to showcase more of the frame. This is particularly important for a character like Superman, whose story often involves vast, sweeping landscapes and high-altitude perspectives. The film's flight sequences, for instance, are expected to leverage the full verticality of the IMAX frame, giving audiences a bird's-eye view of both Smallville's pastoral beauty and Metropolis's urban sprawl. These sequences are not just about spectacle but about placing the audience in Superman's shoes, allowing them to experience the exhilaration of flight firsthand.

Another key feature of IMAX is its superior image resolution and color fidelity. Superman (2025) has reportedly been shot using state-of-the-art digital cameras capable of capturing high dynamic range (HDR) imagery. This technology ensures that the film's visuals are rich in detail and texture, from the intricate designs of Kryptonian artifacts to the subtle expressions on the characters' faces. The use of HDR also enhances the film's lighting effects, making Superman's heat vision and other energy-based powers visually striking without feeling overblown or artificial.

Sound design is another area where IMAX excels, and it plays a crucial role in amplifying the impact of the film's visuals. The IMAX sound system's precision and dynamic range ensure that every sonic detail, from the hum of Kryptonian machinery to the thunderous impact of a mid-air collision, is rendered with crystal clarity. The combination of immersive visuals and a powerful soundscape creates a multi-sensory experience that draws the audience deeper into the story.

The IMAX format also enhances the film's emotional beats. James Gunn is known for his ability to weave humor, pathos, and grandeur into his storytelling, and IMAX provides the ideal canvas for these elements to shine. Whether it's an intimate conversation between Clark Kent and Lois Lane or a climactic battle against overwhelming odds, the format's immersive qualities ensure that these moments resonate deeply with the audience. The sheer scale of the IMAX screen magnifies the characters' emotions, making their struggles and triumphs feel larger than life.

Bridging Spectacle and Emotion

What sets Superman (2025) apart is its commitment to using visuals not just as a means of spectacle but as a storytelling tool. The special effects and IMAX presentation work in tandem to bridge the gap between Superman's superhuman abilities and his human vulnerabilities. This duality is central to the character's appeal, and the film's visual approach reflects this complexity.

For example, the contrast between Krypton's advanced, otherworldly aesthetic and the humble simplicity of Smallville is rendered with striking clarity. The vibrant, hyper-detailed landscapes of Krypton highlight the grandeur of Superman's heritage, while the warm, earthy tones of Smallville underscore the humanity that defines his moral compass. This visual dichotomy serves to reinforce the film's central theme: the struggle to reconcile two identities and find a sense of belonging.

Moreover, the film's use of visual effects extends to its portrayal of Superman's internal struggles. Subtle visual cues, such as the interplay of light and shadow on his face or the way his cape moves in response to his mood, add layers of depth to the character. These details might go unnoticed on a standard screen, but in IMAX, they become part of the audience's emotional experience.

The visuals and effects in Superman (2025) are poised to set a new benchmark for superhero cinema. By combining cutting-edge technology with a deep understanding of the character's essence, the film promises to deliver a visual experience that is as emotionally resonant as it is spectacular. The focus on special effects ensures that Superman's world feels both awe-inspiring and grounded, while the IMAX presentation amplifies every detail, creating an immersive journey that captures the imagination. As audiences prepare to soar alongside the Man of Steel, one thing is clear: Superman (2025) is not just a movie; it's a cinematic event.

Chapter 5

Role in the DC Universe: Chapter One: Gods and Monsters

Superman holds a unique place in the history of comic books and cinema, serving as a beacon of hope, justice, and heroism. With James Gunn's Superman: Legacy, scheduled for release on July 11, 2025, the character's cinematic journey is set to take on a pivotal role in rebooting the DC Universe (DCU) under a new creative direction. This film is not merely an exploration of Superman as a character but is the cornerstone of DC's Chapter One: "Gods and Monsters," a thematic narrative arc that redefines the cinematic world of DC Comics. By establishing this chapter, the film aspires to integrate Superman into a broader, interconnected universe while paying homage to his legacy.

Chapter One: Gods and Monsters

The designation of the new DCU's first chapter as "Gods and Monsters" is a testament to the expansive and layered storytelling vision of James Gunn and his team. This title evokes the duality that has always been inherent in superhero narratives: the godlike powers of heroes and the monstrous adversities they must confront. Within this framework, Superman emerges as a linchpin, embodying the tension between divine potential and human morality.

In previous cinematic outings, Superman has been portrayed both as an invincible savior and a flawed being grappling with his place in the world. In Gunn's vision, Superman: Legacy promises to delve deeper into these dualities, emphasizing Clark Kent's struggle to reconcile his Kryptonian heritage with his human upbringing. This thematic exploration aligns perfectly with the "Gods and Monsters" ethos, showcasing the humanity behind the myth and the choices that define greatness.

Furthermore, by placing Superman at the center of this thematic chapter, the film aims to set a philosophical tone for the entire DCU. It suggests a universe where power is not merely a means to an end but a responsibility laden with moral and ethical dilemmas. This layered storytelling has the potential to elevate superhero films beyond spectacle, offering narratives that resonate on a profound emotional level.

Rebooting the Franchise

The decision to reboot the DCU comes in the wake of a series of mixed critical and commercial responses to prior DC films. While some, like Wonder Woman (2017) and Aquaman (2018), achieved success, others struggled to find their footing, leading to a fragmented and inconsistent cinematic universe. With Superman: Legacy, James Gunn and producer Peter Safran aim to reset the narrative landscape, crafting a unified and coherent vision for the DCU.

Rebooting the franchise through Superman is a strategic move that acknowledges the character's cultural significance. As the first superhero in comic book history, Superman's legacy serves as a symbolic starting point for a new era. By reintroducing him to audiences in a way that balances classic elements with fresh perspectives, Gunn seeks to honor the character's storied past while making him relevant for contemporary viewers.

This reboot also provides an opportunity to establish a cohesive tone and aesthetic for the DCU. Superman's optimistic worldview and moral clarity can serve as a blueprint for other characters and storylines within the universe. By presenting a hero who leads with compassion and integrity, Superman: Legacy could set a standard for the kind of stories the DCU wants to tell, creating a foundation that resonates across multiple films and series.

Integration with Other DC Properties

Another critical aspect of Superman's role in rebooting the franchise lies in his integration with other DC characters. As the inaugural film of "Gods and Monsters," Superman: Legacy is expected to introduce or hint at other heroes and villains who will play significant roles in the DCU. This interconnected approach mirrors the successful formula employed by rival franchises, creating a shared universe that encourages audiences to invest in multiple storylines.

For instance, Superman's interactions with characters like Batman, Wonder Woman, and Green Lantern could pave the way for a cohesive Justice League narrative. Additionally, the film might explore connections to lesser-known characters, expanding the DCU's scope and providing opportunities for diverse storytelling. By positioning Superman as a unifying figure, the DCU can establish a sense of continuity and shared purpose among its characters.

Challenges and Opportunities

Rebooting the DCU through Superman also comes with significant challenges. One of the primary concerns is managing audience expectations. Superman has been portrayed by numerous actors over the years, each bringing their unique interpretation to the role. From Christopher Reeve's iconic performance to Henry Cavill's modern portrayal, audiences have developed strong attachments to specific versions of the character. As a result, David Corenswet, the actor stepping into the role for Superman: Legacy, faces the daunting task of meeting these expectations while carving out his own legacy.

Additionally, the film must strike a balance between honoring the source material and offering a fresh perspective. Superman's story has been told and retold countless times, and audiences may be wary of yet another origin story or a rehash of familiar themes. To overcome this, Gunn's script will need to emphasize character depth and thematic richness, focusing on aspects of Superman's journey that have not been thoroughly explored in previous adaptations.

On the other hand, the reboot presents numerous opportunities. With advancements in visual effects and storytelling techniques, Superman: Legacy can deliver a cinematic experience that captures the awe-inspiring nature of Superman's powers while grounding his story in emotional realism. Furthermore, the film's position as the starting point of a new DCU allows it to take creative risks, setting a precedent for innovation and bold storytelling within the franchise.

Establishing a Legacy

Ultimately, the success of Superman: Legacy will hinge on its ability to resonate with audiences on both an emotional and intellectual level. By positioning Superman as the moral and thematic anchor of the DCU, the film has the potential to redefine the character's legacy for a new generation. More than just a reboot, it represents a chance to explore what makes Superman timeless: his unwavering belief in the goodness of humanity and his commitment to using his powers for the greater good.

As the first chapter in "Gods and Monsters," Superman: Legacy carries the weight of setting the tone for an entire cinematic universe. If successful, it could not only restore faith in the DC brand but also redefine what superhero films can achieve. By embracing the complexity of its characters and themes, the film has the opportunity to inspire audiences and establish a legacy that endures for years to come.

Chapter 6

Anticipation and First Impressions

The anticipation surrounding the upcoming Superman film, scheduled for release on July 11, 2025, is immense. With James Gunn at the helm, the movie promises to reboot the iconic superhero franchise, ushering in a new era for Superman within the larger DC Universe. The excitement is palpable not only because of the film's ties to the long-standing legacy of Superman but also due to the fresh direction that Gunn, known for his work on Guardians of the Galaxy and The Suicide Squad, brings to the project. In this essay, we will explore the teaser trailer breakdown, examining the first impressions it leaves on audiences, and how these visuals shape the expectations for the film.

Teaser Trailer Breakdown

When the teaser trailer for Superman dropped in December 2024, it created a wave of excitement across social media, with fans and critics alike dissecting every frame for clues about the movie's direction. Unlike previous trailers for

Superman films, which often emphasize explosive action sequences or larger-than-life battles, this teaser took a more intimate and emotional approach. Set against a backdrop of a quiet and nostalgic Smallville, we see Clark Kent in his early stages of self-discovery, struggling to balance his Kryptonian origins with his human upbringing.

The first few moments of the trailer are understated and serene. Clark Kent, portrayed by David Corenswet, is seen standing alone in a field, looking up at the sky with a sense of longing. This quiet moment sets the tone for the film, suggesting a Superman who is deeply introspective, grappling with the duality of his identity. The trailer then transitions into glimpses of his life in Smallville, showcasing his adoptive parents, Jonathan and Martha Kent, and the bonds Clark shares with the people of Earth. These shots highlight the importance of Superman's human side—an aspect often overshadowed by his god-like powers in past films.

As the teaser progresses, we get a few action shots that hint at the scale of the movie. A brief, fast-paced sequence of Superman soaring through the sky, followed by flashes of his heat vision, hints at the epic nature of the film. However, these moments are brief, reinforcing the idea that while Superman is indeed a superhero, the film's primary focus is on his human emotions, relationships, and internal struggles. This nuanced approach to the character is what sets Superman apart from its predecessors, which often leaned into action-heavy storytelling.

One of the most striking moments in the trailer is the brief but powerful appearance of Superman's iconic "S" symbol. The symbol, which stands for hope in Kryptonian culture, is shown subtly throughout the trailer, reinforcing the film's thematic emphasis on hope, justice, and the personal growth of Clark Kent as he comes to terms with his place in the world. This imagery, along with the emotional beats, helps ground the film in the heart of Superman's character rather than focusing solely on spectacle.

The teaser's music further complements the tone, with a soft orchestral score building in intensity as the visuals unfold. The music, combined with the emotional undercurrent of the trailer, draws the audience in and heightens the anticipation for what is to come. The decision to hold back on revealing too much about the plot is a clever one, allowing the audience to speculate while ensuring they remain invested in the film's emotional journey.

Audience Expectations

The release of the teaser trailer has sparked widespread discussion and raised a number of expectations among the audience. Fans of the Superman franchise are particularly eager to see how the new film will honor the character's legacy while introducing a fresh take. James Gunn's involvement as director has garnered considerable attention, as his style is known for blending humor, heart, and emotional depth, as seen in his previous works with Marvel and DC. Many fans are hopeful that Gunn's approach will breathe new life into the Superman character, who, over the years, has become more of an emblem of invulnerability than a relatable, flawed hero.

One of the primary expectations stemming from the trailer is the emphasis on Clark Kent's internal conflict. Previous iterations of Superman have often focused on his role as a protector of humanity, leaving little room for his struggles with identity and vulnerability. The teaser, however, presents Superman as a more humanized character, one who questions his place in the world and faces emotional turmoil as he learns to embrace both his Kryptonian heritage and his Earthly upbringing. This focus on character development has piqued the interest of fans who want to see a Superman who is not just a superhero but a person, struggling to find his place in a world that demands perfection.

Another key expectation is the film's exploration of Superman's relationships with key characters, such as Lois Lane, portrayed by Rachel Brosnahan. While the teaser offers only brief glimpses of Lois, the chemistry between her and Clark is expected to be a central part of the story. Superman's relationship with Lois has always been one of the most enduring aspects of his character, and audiences are eager to see how this dynamic will be handled in the new film. Will Lois be portrayed as more than just a love interest, or will she have a more active role in shaping Superman's journey? The trailer hints that Lois will be an important figure in Clark's emotional growth, but it remains to be seen how this relationship will unfold.

The appearance of Lex Luthor, portrayed by Nicholas Hoult, also raises questions about how he will be depicted in the new film. Luthor has been a central antagonist in Superman's history, but the teaser keeps his role under wraps, leaving fans to wonder whether he will be portrayed as a more personal foe for Clark or whether his character will serve as a broader representation of the challenges Superman faces in accepting his power. Luthor's presence in the trailer is limited to just a few seconds, which only adds to the mystery surrounding his involvement.

As with any superhero film, there are high expectations surrounding the film's visual effects. The teaser provided a taste of what's to come, with shots of Superman flying through the sky and using his heat vision. These moments, though brief, suggest that the film will have spectacular visuals, but what sets Superman apart is its commitment to balancing these action sequences with emotional depth. The decision to focus more on the character's internal struggles than on the visual spectacle suggests that the film will cater to both long-time fans of Superman and newcomers alike, offering a more layered experience than the typical superhero blockbuster.

Finally, there is anticipation surrounding the film's place in the broader DC Universe. As the inaugural film in the new DC Universe's Chapter One: Gods and Monsters, Superman is expected to set the stage for future films and storylines. This means that while the film will focus on Superman's personal journey, it will also lay the groundwork for the interconnected universe that Gunn has promised. Fans are excited to see how this new vision for the DC Universe will take shape, especially after the mixed reactions to earlier DCEU films.

In conclusion, the Superman movie, set for release in 2025, is surrounded by high expectations, largely due to the new direction brought by James Gunn. The teaser trailer has given audiences a glimpse of the film's emotional depth, focusing on Superman's internal struggles and relationships rather than just its action-packed moments. The first impressions are clear: this film aims to redefine Superman as a more humanized, vulnerable hero, while also providing the spectacle that fans have come to expect. With a talented cast, a fresh take on the character, and an emotionally resonant story, the anticipation for Superman continues to grow as we approach its release.

conclusion

The excitement surrounding the 2025 Superman film directed by James Gunn is palpable, with fans eagerly awaiting the return of the iconic superhero to the big screen. As one of the most beloved and powerful characters in comic book history, Superman's legacy is inextricably linked to the evolution of the superhero genre itself. With Gunn's distinct vision and a fresh direction for the DC Universe, there are numerous reasons why this film holds the potential to redefine the character and further solidify Superman's place in modern cinematic storytelling.

Summary of Excitement for the Film

The announcement of a new Superman film, particularly after the conclusion of the DCEU's previous iterations, has generated a wave of anticipation. James Gunn, known for his work on the Guardians of the Galaxy series and The Suicide Squad, brings a unique touch to superhero storytelling, blending humor, heart, and spectacle. His approach to Superman marks a departure from the darker, grittier tone of previous films, aiming to bring the character back to his roots of hope, optimism, and inspiration. This shift has been widely welcomed by fans who are eager to see a Superman that is both powerful and human, capable of inspiring the world around him.

David Corenswet, cast as Clark Kent/Superman, has already generated excitement with his portrayal of the iconic role. Corenswet's physical presence, coupled with his ability to capture the moral complexity of Superman, promises to bring a fresh yet familiar take on the character. Rachel Brosnahan's casting as Lois Lane also adds to the excitement, as her strong acting chops promise to bring a grounded, relatable Lois to life, one who will be more than just a love interest. Nicholas Hoult's turn as Lex Luthor, as the film's primary antagonist, adds another layer of anticipation, as fans are eager to see how this version of Luthor will challenge Superman's ideals.

Moreover, the decision to focus on Superman's internal struggle, as he grapples with his Kryptonian heritage and his human upbringing, is one of the most compelling aspects of the film. This will allow the audience to see a more vulnerable and emotionally nuanced version of Superman, making him a more relatable and complex hero. The first teaser trailer, which showcases this theme of vulnerability, has further fueled fan excitement, offering a glimpse into the heart of the story and the emotional stakes for the character.

The fact that the film is set to be part of the new DC Universe's Chapter One: Gods and Monsters is another reason for heightened anticipation. Gunn's plans for the DCU promise a cohesive, interconnected universe, and Superman will play a pivotal role in shaping its future. Fans are eager to see how this new version of Superman will interact with other key characters in the universe and how his story will be integrated into the larger narrative. The idea of a Superman who is both a symbol of hope and an anchor for a new era of superhero films has sparked considerable enthusiasm.

Predictions for Impact on the Superman Legacy

As the first major superhero to make the jump from comic book pages to film, Superman has long held a place of prominence in the world of cinema. From the groundbreaking 1978 Superman: The Movie, starring Christopher Reeve, to the more recent portrayals by Henry Cavill, Superman's legacy has been defined by moments of grandeur, vulnerability, and the ever-present struggle between good and evil. The 2025 film, under Gunn's direction, has the potential to impact the Superman legacy in profound ways.

One of the most significant impacts this film will have is the re-establishment of Superman as a symbol of hope and optimism. After years of darker, more cynical portrayals of superheroes in popular media, this new Superman film has the potential to reinvigorate the character and reintroduce him as a beacon of positivity in a world that desperately needs it. By focusing on Superman's humanity and the timeless theme of doing good, no matter the cost, the film can restore the character's place as a cultural icon of justice, morality, and selflessness.

Moreover, the film's approach to Superman's internal conflict and personal growth will likely resonate with modern audiences, especially as superhero stories continue to evolve and mature. In an era where audiences crave deeper, more complex characters, this new portrayal of Superman promises to offer a hero who is not just an unstoppable force, but a relatable individual who struggles with his own identity and place in the world. The exploration of Clark Kent's journey, balancing his Kryptonian legacy with his human upbringing, is a theme that can transcend the comic book genre and offer something meaningful to a broad audience.

The film also has the potential to impact how Superman is perceived in relation to other superheroes. With a new, cohesive DC Universe being launched, this Superman will serve as the cornerstone for future films and character arcs. Fans will likely see the ripple effects of this film in future Justice League movies, where Superman's role as a leader, a symbol, and a moral compass will be more pronounced than ever before. His legacy, grounded in hope and determination, will undoubtedly influence the tone and direction of other DC films.

Finally, with James Gunn at the helm, the 2025 Superman film is poised to leave a lasting legacy in the world of superhero filmmaking. Known for his ability to craft emotionally resonant stories without sacrificing spectacle, Gunn has the potential to elevate the Superman mythos to new heights. Whether through captivating action sequences, rich character development, or compelling narrative choices, Gunn's Superman promises to be a defining chapter in both the character's history and the future of superhero cinema.

In conclusion, the 2025 Superman film offers much more than just a new take on the Man of Steel. It promises to restore Superman to his rightful place as a symbol of hope, while also bringing a fresh, modern approach to his character. With the talent behind the film and the anticipation building, there's no doubt that this new Superman will have a profound impact on both the character's legacy and the broader world of superhero films. Fans can only hope that the film lives up to its potential and cements Superman's place as a timeless hero for a new generation.

Made in the USA
Las Vegas, NV
18 April 2025